Out in th

Jenny Giles
Illustrated by Kristine Dresen

It is a rainy day.

Look at us.

It is a cloudy day.

Look at us.

It is a windy day.

Look at us.

It is a frosty day.

Look at us.

It is a snowy day.

Look at us.

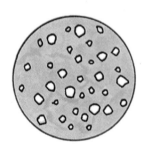

It is a stormy day.

Look at us.

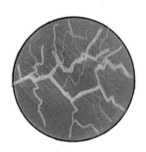

It is a sunny day ...

Look at us!

The Pithead Baths S

National Museum Wales Books

First published in 2010 by National Museum Wales Books, Cathays Park, Cardiff, CF10 3NP, Wales.

© the National Museum of Wales

ISBN 978 0 7200 0608 7

Text: Gareth Salway and Ceri Thompson
Design: Peter Gill & Associates
Editing: Mari Gordon
Welsh language edition available,
Hanes y Baddondai Pen Pwll
ISBN 978 0 7200 0609 4

Contents

Introduction

It is difficult today to imagine the great impact that the introduction of pithead baths had on coalmining communities. They brought improvements in health to both the mineworkers and their families, and changed the way these communities were perceived by the world outside the coalfields.

Before pithead baths

A midwife of 23 years' experience in the same district in the Rhondda stated to me that the majority of cases of premature births and extreme female ailments are due to the physical strain of lifting heavy tubs and boilers in their homes.
Coal Industry Commission, 1919

Before pithead baths became widely available, most coalminers, already exhausted from a day's work, had little choice but to travel home still filthy with coal dust. Their clothing was often soaked with sweat and water and they were often at risk of contracting pneumonia, bronchitis or rheumatism.

Once home they had the task of removing as much of the dirt as possible in a tin bath in front of the fire, often taking their turn with other members of the household who were also miners. There was usually a hierarchy to this, as a Rhymney miner, born in 1881, remembered:

…they would bath their top half first and their bottom half after, from the senior member down. Usually the Dad first, then the eldest son and then down the line – the youngest son was always last.

The women of the house were responsible for heating the water for the miners' baths and cleaning and drying their clothes. There was also the constant battle to clean the house of the all-prevailing coal dust. This was never-ending, backbreaking work; exhaustion and physical strain often led to serious health problems, and in some cases to miscarriages or premature births.

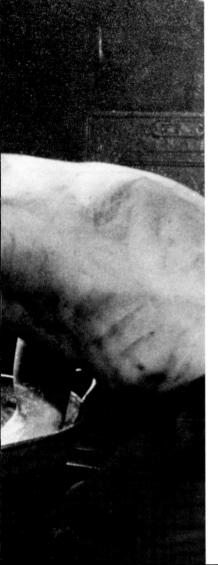

The sheer quantity of hot water used in the miners' homes was also very dangerous in itself; one south Wales coroner claimed: 'Every winter I hold more inquests on miners' children who die from scalds or burns than I do on miners who are killed underground.'

In spite of the problems, it took considerable lobbying by social reformers, working under the banner of the Pithead Baths Movement, to convince the Government, mine-owners, and even some of the miners and their wives, that pithead baths were needed. From the initial campaigns of the 1890s it was a long, hard struggle to eventually achieve a special fund for the building of baths in 1926, under the auspices of the Miners' Welfare Committee.

John Davies of Ferndale washes in a tin bath while his baby daughter, Marianne, looks on.

9

The first pithead baths in Wales

Pithead baths had been in use in Belgium, France and Germany since the 1880s. In 1913 David Davies, the proprietor of the Ocean Coal Company who famously became known as 'Davies the Ocean', sent a delegation to see these European baths. This visit led to the building of the first Welsh baths at Deep Navigation Colliery, Treharris, in 1916. The success of the baths here played a key part in the campaign to have pithead baths at every Welsh colliery.

The Sankey Commission

In 1919 the British Government established a Royal Commission, known as the Sankey Commission, to investigate social and living conditions in the coalfields. As a result a Miners' Welfare Fund was set up to '…improve the social wellbeing, recreation, and condition of living of workers in or about coalmines.' The fund gained its income through a levy of a penny on every ton of coal mined. It was used for various purposes, including the provision of playing fields, swimming pools, libraries and institutes. From 1926 an additional levy was raised specifically to fund a baths-building programme.

During the existence of the Miners' Welfare Fund, from 1921 to 1952, over 400 pithead baths were built in Britain.

Overleaf: The first pithead baths in Wales at Deep Navigation Colliery, Treharris, 1916.

OCEAN COLLIERY

THS,   TREHARRIS.

Opening Ceremony

ON THE 28TH JANUARY, 1939.

Order of Proceedings:—

W. E. Rouzel, Esq., Chairman of the Management Committee, will take the chair at 3-15 p.m.

Short Speeches will be made by—

J. H. Lones, Esq., J.P., Director of the Blaenavon Company Limited.

Obadiah Evans, Esq., J.P., Miners' Agent.

W. L. Cook, Esq., O.B.E., J.P., Miners' Welfare Committee, London, will hand over the Buildings to the Baths Trustees, supported by W. M. Taylor, Esq., I.R.I.B.A.

W. E. Rouzel, Esq., will accept same on behalf of the Trustees, supported by S. Banks, Esq.

Mrs. J. H. Lones will then open the Baths.

IN CANTEEN:—

E. Hutchings, Esq., will propose a vote of thanks to Mrs. J. H. Lones, seconded by F. W. Gratton, Esq.

PRESENTATION TO MRS. J. H. LONES.

TO BE FOLLOWED BY TEA, WHICH WILL BE SERVED AT THE WELFARE HALL, FORGESIDE.

G. H. Simpson, Esq., will take the chair.

Short Speeches will be made by:—

Major Armstrong, Arthur Jenkins, Esq. M.P.,
C. Humphreys, Esq., A. H. Horner, Esq.,
C. Sullivan, Esq., Rt. Hon. William Brace, P.C.,
W. Frowen, Esq., O.B.E., J.P.

After the ceremony, the Baths will be open for inspection by the public until 7 p.m., and on the Sunday, the 29th instant, from 2-30 p.m. to 5 p.m. Ladies specially invited.

On Saturday evening, January 28th, a Dance will be held at the Welfare Hall, Forgeside. Tickets, 1/- each. M.C.'s: W. E. Rouzel, Esq., and W. Davies, Esq. Dancing from 7-30 p.m. to 11-30 p.m.

Big Pit

TH

The Baths h
Committee out
up of a levy of
is the Output
and reduced to
£1 of royalties
Royalties Welfa
Royalties Welfa
upon providing
Output Levy sut

The site of
the Trustees, by

The Baths
property include
on it, and any n
to or invested
rules for the ma

Four Truste
the Colliery, and

The Truste
Pithead Baths.
any) of the si
vision for the
workman being

They are a
all income and
out annually an

...iery Pithead Baths.

...gin of the Baths.

...n built by the Central Miners' Welfare
...Miners' Welfare Fund, which is made
...of the output of every coal mine (this
...Levy instituted at 1d. a ton in 1921
...n in 1934) and a levy of 1s. for every
...n the production of coal (this is the
...instituted in 1926). The whole of the
...y is required by law to be expended
...l baths, together with a part of the
...to make up £375,000 a year.

...lding has been provided, or secured to
...ners of the Colliery.

...e Baths Trust.

...en constituted as a trust, of which the
...Baths site, together with the buildings
...and investments or other property paid
...Trustees. The Trust Deed contains
...nt of the Baths.

...e been appointed, two by the owners of
...the workmen employed at the Colliery.

...the trust property for the purposes of
...are responsible for paying the rent (if
...for insuring the Baths, including pro-
...nt of compensation in the event of a
...l on the trust premises.

...ponsible for keeping proper accounts of
...diture. A balance sheet will be made
...ed up in the Baths.

The 'architects of modernism'

*Huge washing machines in which
dirty miners went in one end and
clean ones out the other...*
Bert Coombes

The architects' department of
the Miners' Welfare Committee
established the most cost-effective
way of constructing, equipping
and operating baths buildings.
By the 1930s a 'house style'
had developed, based on the
International Modern Movement of
architectural design.

The pithead baths were designed
to create an atmosphere of health
and brightness. They stood out
among other colliery buildings,
with their flat, clean lines and
plentiful use of glass. The use of
light, especially natural light, was
deemed important not only to
aid cleaning and hygiene, but to
create an atmosphere of health
and brightness — very important for
miners who had just spent a shift in
poor light underground.

One of the key principles of the design was to separate the clean and dirty sections of the building so that dirty miners and their working clothes were kept apart from miners who had washed and were wearing their clean, home clothes.

Some baths, such as the one at Big Pit, were rendered white which, even today, makes it a prominent landmark on the hillside. The pithead baths at Big Pit were opened on 28 January 1939; they were one of fifty-two British baths opened during that year – a record for the Miners' Welfare Committee. By then south Wales had forty-one baths, providing facilities for over 54,000 mineworkers. However the Miners' Welfare Committee had limited resources, and many Welsh collieries were not provided with baths until the 1950s.

Penallta Colliery Pithead baths, opened in 1938.

The baths were not just places to wash, they also included medical and canteen facilities. When the National Coal Board took over the responsibility for pithead baths after 1947, they usually installed medical centres to replace the former first-aid rooms. Medical centres were often staffed by a state registered nurse although at Big Pit the centre was staffed by qualified medical attendants.

Caerau Colliery Pithead baths, opened in 1954.

The Canteen

Big Pit canteen was always very clean. It was run by local women working for the NCB. They all seemed quite elderly – but I was young at the time! The manageress was Mrs Jones; she ran it with a rod of iron – you couldn't swear, couldn't come in with dirty boots and if you tipped your tea – God help you!
Jeff White, Big Pit

Big Pit's canteen was initially designed to provide hot drinks and light snacks rather than full meals. But it wasn't only tea and cakes that were available…

Big Pit canteen, 1970s.

The canteen was the best place to find out gossip about Blaenafon – the girls always seemed to know what was going on. The tea was drinkable – if you were desperate! The stuff on sale was pretty basic – soap, towels, slab cake, pasties, chewing tobacco, snuff etc. and you could also buy Tommy (food) boxes and water jacks – Oh, and 'Noso'!

John Perrett, Big Pit

Noso was a popular product sold in the canteens. It was a white, rubbery liquid with a strong, pungent smell, used to carry out repairs on working clothes. A workman would take a patch of material covered with Noso and place it over the rip to make a rough and ready repair without recourse to a needle and cotton.

Big Pit canteen, 1970s.

Because men were forbidden to smoke underground, the canteen sold chewing tobacco. A packet was often purchased between two miners, the usual agreement being that one would cut the length in half and the other would choose which piece he wanted. Chewing tobacco was known as 'twist' or 'screw'. Many young miners found amusement in asking the canteen girls 'Can I have a screw please?'

It was also possible to buy good-quality towels and other items for the home – even babies' nappies!

After 1947 food and drink were served on crockery bearing the National Coal Board logo. The tea mugs were huge and made from thick china, which led to the expression 'He's really stupid – as thick as a canteen cup!'

'Canteen girls', Taff Merthyr Colliery, c.1979.

The Locker Rooms

The lockers always seemed crowded in the 1960s but, by the late 1970s, the pit was running down and there was more room; by then I had wangled three lockers for myself – more space to dry my work clothes!
John Scandrett, Big Pit

There were two locker rooms – a 'dirty' ('pit') locker room to house the men's working clothes and a 'clean' locker room for their home clothes. At Big Pit each locker room was designed to hold 792 numbered lockers. Men were supposed to be allocated lockers in a way that avoided congestion at peak periods of baths use. However, this proposed system often proved unworkable in reality, and locker rooms could be very chaotic at times.

By J. Armstrong   Seahe

Left: The 'dirty side' lockers at Big Pit, 1970s.

Above: A cartoon from *Coal News*.

Big Pit pithead baths – dirty miners going in…

...and clean ones coming out!

The Bath House (Shower Room)

The Big Pit baths were always immaculate – you couldn't fault the cleanliness – second to none.
John Perrett, Big Pit

The bath house was designed to bath a shift of several hundred men (using around six gallons of hot water each) in something like thirty minutes. In addition, the resultant waste water had to be disposed of, adding to an already formidable engineering feat!

There were seventy-eight showers at Big Pit with each cubicle originally provided with a canvas curtain for privacy. These curtains seemed to have gone out of use soon after the baths opened. Each cubicle was provided with a polished steel mirror and hooks to hang towels etc.

The shower cubicles were colour-coded – blue or red – to match the coloured numbers on the locker doors. Men were instructed to use cubicles that matched the colour on their lockers. However, it is unlikely that the system worked in practice as there was always a mad rush for the nearest shower in order to get home as quickly as possible.

A shower cubicle at Big Pit, complete with colour code and towel hook.

Cwm Colliery, 1970s.

There are difficult places to reach with a flannel, and the *Big Pit Bather's Handbook* of 1939 advises bathers to: 'Get your "butty" to wash your back. Then you do his. The most up-to-date installation has not yet discovered any better method of "back-washing".'

'Get your butty to wash your back!'

Other rooms

The bottle-filling room
As no drinking water was provided underground, the miners had to carry their own. Glass bottles were forbidden as they could break in the locker and bath areas and cause possible injury to men who were barefooted.

Toilets
The original lavatories at Big Pit consist of three toilet cubicles – without doors! – and a urinal. There were no byelaws for the toilets at Big Pit, but Cambrian Colliery baths handbook states that 'Standing on lavatory seats is strictly forbidden.'

The bottle filling room at Big Pit, 1970s.

The boot-cleaning room
This room contained boot-cleaning machines. Boots were not supposed to be brushed after greasing, an order that was often ignored by young miners who wanted to see how shiny they could get them!

The boot-greasing room
Grease was applied to working boots to waterproof them. Boots were only to be greased immediately before leaving the building, so that the grease wasn't carried into the locker rooms.

Left: The boot-cleaning room at Penallta Colliery, 1938.

41

Staff

The baths at Big Pit was staffed by a superintendent and two attendants – four in the 1950s when the baths was extended. Baths staff were responsible for maintaining the equipment, keeping the building clean and maintaining discipline among the users.

Much of the attendants' time was spent cleaning the building. The bath house was cleaned after each shift had bathed. It was especially important to clean the cubicle areas, because if the mixture of soap and coal dust was allowed to dry it became as hard as cement! Big Pit was one of eight baths congratulated by the Miners' Welfare Committee in 1939 for its high standards.

The rules

The rules for using the baths were posted on noticeboards throughout the building. They regulated how the baths were to be used and emphasised the need for discipline and orderly behaviour. Sharp tools or glass were not to be brought into the baths; running, smoking and entering the clean locker room in dirty clothes were all forbidden. Anyone who disobeyed the rules was excluded from using the baths, as were men suffering from an infectious or contagious disease, in particular Athlete's Foot.

At war

The Second World War had an impact on the operation of pithead baths. The blackout regulations meant that all the large glass windows had to be painted out, which increased the lighting costs. Wartime conditions also prevented much of the usual maintenance, meaning that many baths were in poor condition by 1945.

There were manpower shortages as men were called up for military service, although the Government gave concessions to enable miners to obtain towels and soap, and attendants to obtain rubber boots. In addition, rather than give miners extra rations at home, canteens were provided with extra food for them at work.

Today

In our little valley
They closed the colliery down,
And the pithead baths is a
supermarket now.
Empty journeys red with rust roll to
rest among the dust
And the pithead baths is a
supermarket now.
Duw it's hard, Max Boyce: Live at
Treorchy (1973)

Although a few survive as offices
or light engineering works, most
pithead baths, along with the
collieries they once served,
have now been demolished. The
ground they occupied has been
redeveloped to provide new
employment and amenities for the
communities the mining created.

In 2007 however the Welsh public
showed that they had not forgotten
these iconic buildings, when BBC2
viewers voted the pithead baths at
Big Pit 'Wales's Favourite National
Treasure'.

Max Boyce by his locker at Big Pit.

For more information on the
coal industry visit
Big Pit: National Coal Museum,
Blaenafon, Torfaen NP4 9XP
Tel. (01495) 790311

Find out more about Big Pit and all
Wales's national museums at
www.museumwales.ac.uk.

For more great books and gifts
visit our online shop at
www.museumwales.ac.uk/shop.

National Museum Wales Books
is the publishing imprint of
Amgueddfa Cymru – National
Museum Wales.